MW00785032

America's BEST LOVED HYMNS
Collection Three

Let Us Praise God for All He Has Done!

Believers throughout the ages have felt the glorious presence of the Creator as they lift their voices in songs of worship, contrition, and awe. It is the anticipation of that sweet union that inspired authors and musicians to pen the moving stanzas and rousing refrains of these twelve beloved hymns. Although most of these songs were written in the United States, a few of European origin proved so popular they were included in American hymnbooks long ago—and how fortunate we are to count them with our own! Each treasured song in this collection is carefully charted for cross stitch with beautiful images that will lift your spirit as you recreate the design. The story of each song's beginning is also included so that you can relive the joy, solace, and wonder that inspired the writers and composers so many years ago. Display your favorites in your home, or prepare them as thoughtful gifts of love and encouragement.

General Instructions

Working With Charts

How To Read Charts:

Each design is shown in chart form. Each symbol square on the charts represents one Cross Stitch. Colored dots represent French Knots. The straight lines on the charts indicate Backstitch. Complete the Cross Stitches before working Backstitches, and French Knots.

Symbol Key:

The symbol key indicates the color of floss to use for each stitch on the chart. Symbol key columns should be read vertically and horizontally to determine type of stitch and floss color. The following headings are given:

DMC — DMC color number

X — Cross Stitch

FK — French Knot

BS — Backstitch

Stitch Diagrams

When stitching, bring the threaded needle up at 1 and all odd numbers and down at 2 and all even numbers.

Counted Cross Stitch (X):

Work one Cross Stitch to correspond to each symbol square on the chart. For horizontal rows, work stitches in two journeys (Fig. 1). For vertical rows, complete each stitch as shown (Fig. 2).

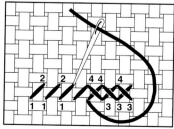

Fig. 1

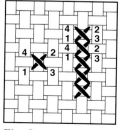

Fig. 2

Backstitch (BS):

For outline detail, Backstitch (shown on chart and on symbol key by colored straight lines) should be worked after the design has been completed (Fig. 3). Stitch with one strand of floss unless otherwise instructed. When the chart shows a Backstitch crossing a symbol square, a Cross Stitch (Fig. 1 or 2) should be worked first, then the Backstitch should be worked on top of the Cross Stitch.

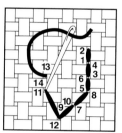

Fig. 3

French Knot (FK):

Bring needle up at 1. Wrap floss once around needle and insert needle at 2, holding end of floss with non-stitching fingers (Fig. 4). Tighten knot, then pull needle through fabric, holding floss until it must be released. Stitch with one strand of floss unless otherwise instructed. For larger knot, use more strands; wrap only once.

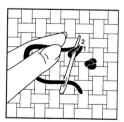

Fig. 4

Stitching Tips

Preparing Fabric

Cut fabric desired size, allowing at least a 3" margin around the design. Overcast raw edges. It is better to waste a little fabric than to come up short after hours of stitching!

Working with Floss

To ensure smoother stitches, separate strands and realign them before threading needle. Keep stitching tension consistent. Begin and end floss by running under several stitches on back; never tie knots.

Dye Lot Variation

It is important to buy all of the floss you need to complete your project from the same dye lot. Although variations in color may be slight, when flosses from two different dye lots are held together, the variation is usually apparent on a stitched piece.

Where to Start

The horizontal and vertical centers of each charted design are shown by arrows. You may start at any point on the charted design, but be sure the design will be centered on the fabric. Locate the center of the fabric by folding in half, top to bottom and again left to right. On the charted design, count the number of squares (stitches) from the center of the chart to where you wish to start. Then from the fabric's center, find your starting point by counting out the same number of fabric threads (stitches).

We Gather Together

Americans know **We Gather Together** as a hymn traditionally sung at Thanksgiving. However, the song was written by an unknown Dutchman in the year 1597 to praise God for his nation's victory over religious oppression. The Netherlands were a battleground during the late sixteenth century, with King Phillip of Spain establishing a reign of terror meant to bring the protestant Dutch back to Roman Catholicism. At the end of the war, the Dutch hymnist gave thanks to the Lord through the words of **We Gather Together** that his people were able to worship as they chose. The song was translated into several European languages, and was eventually translated from German to English in 1894 by Theodore Baker. The song is a rousing reminder to all Christians that God, the one and only true King, provides the ultimate freedom to His children.

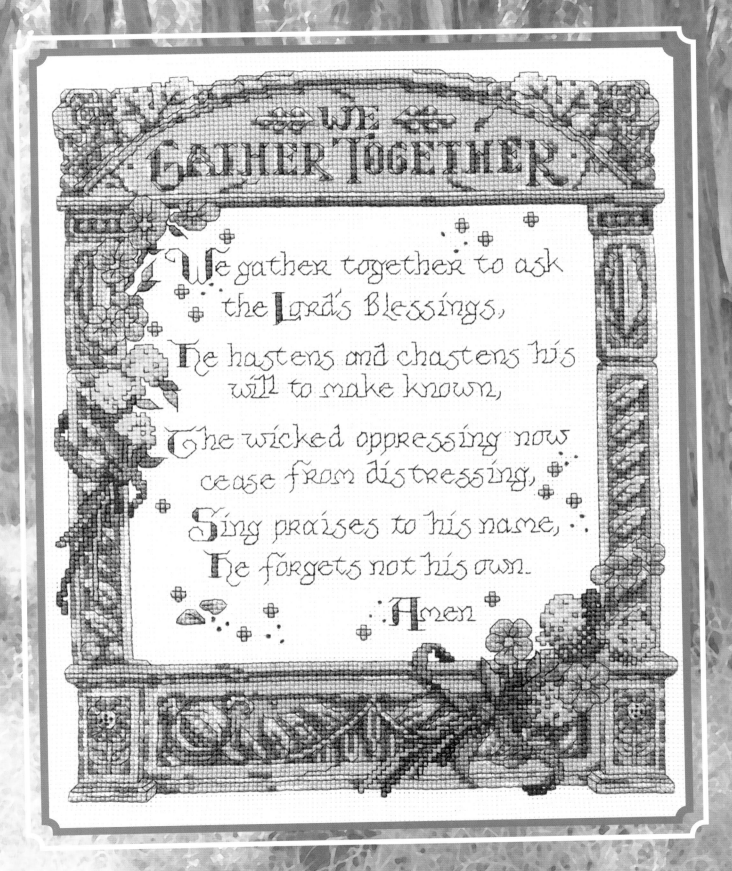

Have Thine Own Way, Lord

Sarah Pollard was born in Iowa during the American Civil War. Never liking the name her parents had given her, Sarah changed her name to Adelaide. Adelaide attended the Boston School of Oratory and moved to Chicago, where she taught in a girls' school. Perhaps due to her frail health, Adelaide was drawn to the ministry of a Scottish-born faith healer who was said to have healed her of diabetes. She followed his teaching for a time, but when his ministry failed, she became deeply involved in the work of an evangelist who proclaimed that Christ's return was imminent. During this time, Adelaide felt called to the mission field of Africa. Bitterly disappointed when she could not raise the necessary support for her mission, Adelaide attended a prayer meeting, where another woman prayed, "It doesn't matter what you bring into our lives, Lord. Just have your own way with us." Adelaide was reminded of the potter in Jeremiah 18. By bedtime that evening, she had written her own prayer, **Have Thine Own Way**. Adelaide did eventually make it to Africa. She also traveled to Scotland and returned to America, where she ministered freely.

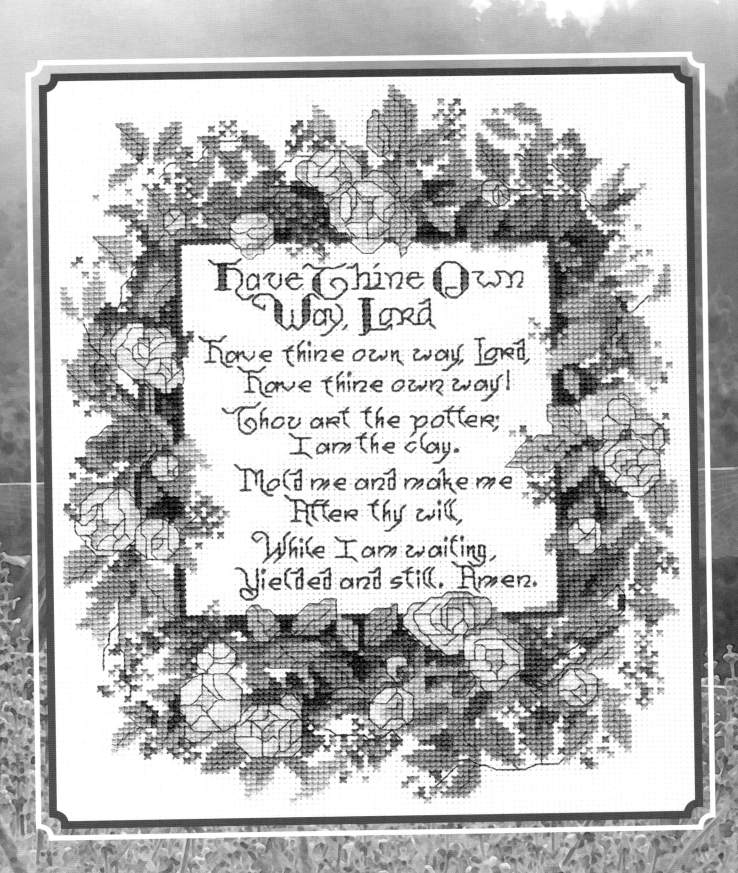

Have Thine Own
Way, Lord

Have thine own way, Lord,
Have thine own way!
Thou art the potter;
I am the clay.
Mold me and make me
After thy will,
While I am waiting,
Yielded and still. Amen.

Go, Tell It on the Mountain

In 1871, John Wesley Work, Jr. was born in Nashville, Tennessee. His father was a church choir director, and John Jr. grew up singing in choirs. When he enrolled in Fisk University, it was natural that young Work became active in its music program. Although he was later hired by the university as a professor of languages, Work's greatest passion was the preservation of the Negro spiritual, a form of American hymnology developed by slaves on American plantations. Like many spirituals of the era, **Go, Tell It on the Mountain** had never been written down; therefore, the words of the stanzas were sometimes obscure. The chorus, however, was clear, upbeat and vibrant. To formalize the song for publishing, Work wrote two additional stanzas. The final version appeared in 1907, in Work's **Folk Songs of the Negro as Sung on the Plantations**, a collection of songs that gave the hope of spiritual freedom to a people who so greatly longed for liberty.

All Things Bright and Beautiful

Mrs. Cecil Frances Alexander was a Sunday school teacher in Ireland who had a special calling to help youngsters understand the Apostles' Creed. Seeing some of the children struggle with the concepts of the creed, she converted portions of it into simple songs the children would enjoy. With Genesis 1:31 as her foundation, she explained the phrase "Maker of heaven and earth" in a song titled **All Things Bright and Beautiful**. Other hymns Mrs. Alexander wrote based on the Apostles' Creed are **Once in Royal David's City**, **There Is a Green Hill Far Away**, and **He Is Coming! He Is Coming!** These hymns were published in 1848 in her book **Hymns for Little Children**, which has been revived in more than 100 editions. Mrs. Alexander was a highly prolific writer, publishing many other books and hymnals, though none exceeded the enormous appeal of her simple, heartfelt compositions based on the Apostles' Creed.

All Things Bright and Beautiful

All things bright and beautiful,
All creatures great and small,

All things wise and wonderful;
The Lord God made them all.

His Eye Is on the Sparrow

Civilla D. Martin and her husband, Walter Stillman Martin, a Baptist minister, were drawn together because of their mutual love for music. Civilla wrote the words for many of the hymns Walter produced. One especially heart-warming song, **His Eye Is on the Sparrow**, was penned by Civilla in 1904 while in the company of a bedridden woman in Elmira, New York. Civilla asked the woman if she sometimes became discouraged by her infirmity. The woman, whose name was Mrs. Doolittle, replied by referencing Matthew 10:29-31, "The Lord's eye is on the sparrow and I know he watches me." Mrs. Doolittle's simple expression of faith touched Civilla's heart. She wrote a poem based on Mrs. Doolittle's words and mailed it to Charles Gabriel, who set it to music. The Martins continued their service to God through ministry and music until their later years, adding several more hymns to their body of work.

His Eye Is On The Sparrow

Why should I feel discouraged,
why should the shadows come

Why should my heart be lonely,
and long for heaven and home.

When Jesus is my portion?
My constant friend is He:

His eye is on the sparrow and I
know He watches me.

I Need Thee Every Hour

On a summer day in 1872, Annie Sherwood Hawks of Brooklyn, New York was doing housework when she suddenly became aware of the intense presence of God. As she later said, "I became so filled with the sense of nearness to the Master that these words—**I Need Thee Every Hour**—took full possession of me." Dr. Robert Lowry set Mrs. Hawks' words to music and added a chorus. The song was published in a hymnbook in 1873. When Annie's husband died several years later, she wrote about the solace she found in her own song. "It was not until the shadow fell over me that I understood something of the comforting power in the words which I had been permitted to give out to others in my hour of sweet serenity and peace."

I NEED THEE
EVERY HOUR

I need thee every hour, Most gracious Lord,
No tender voice like thine Can peace afford.

I need thee, O I need thee,
Every hour I need thee,

O bless me, my Savior,
I came to thee! Amen.

Joyful, Joyful, We Adore Thee

Henry J. Van Dyke was a poet and the author of many devotional writings. Van Dyke was moved by the majesty of the Berkshire mountains in the early 1900s. He found himself pondering all the joyful things in God's creation. The words he wrote to describe these beautiful thoughts were set to music that was previously adapted by Edward Hodges from Ludwig van Beethoven's Ninth Symphony. Van Dyke later wrote, "These verses are simple expressions of common Christian feelings and desires in this present time—hymns of today that may be sung…by people who…are not afraid that any truth of science will destroy religion, or any revolution on earth overthrow the kingdom of heaven. Therefore, this is a hymn of trust and joy and hope."

My Hope Is Built

In the year 1797, Edward Mote was born in London to innkeepers who forbade the presence of a Bible under their roof. Nevertheless, Mote came to Christ as a teenager. Later, the Lord blessed him with work as a carpenter and he eventually owned his own cabinet shop. As Mote began work one day, it occurred to him that he should stop and write a hymn on the "Gracious Experience of a Christian." The now-famous chorus came to him quickly—On Christ the solid rock I stand | All other ground is sinking sand. The following Sabbath, Mote was invited to tea with a fellow believer named King. When he arrived at Mr. King's home, his host shared with him that he was fearful for his wife, who was very ill. Mote offered to sing to the ailing Mrs. King the hymn he had written. She enjoyed the hymn so much that Mote was moved to have a thousand copies printed for distribution. At the age of 55, Edward Mote gave up carpentry to become a church pastor. Shortly before he died, he said, "The truths I have been preaching I am now living upon, and they'll do very well to die upon. Ah! The precious blood."

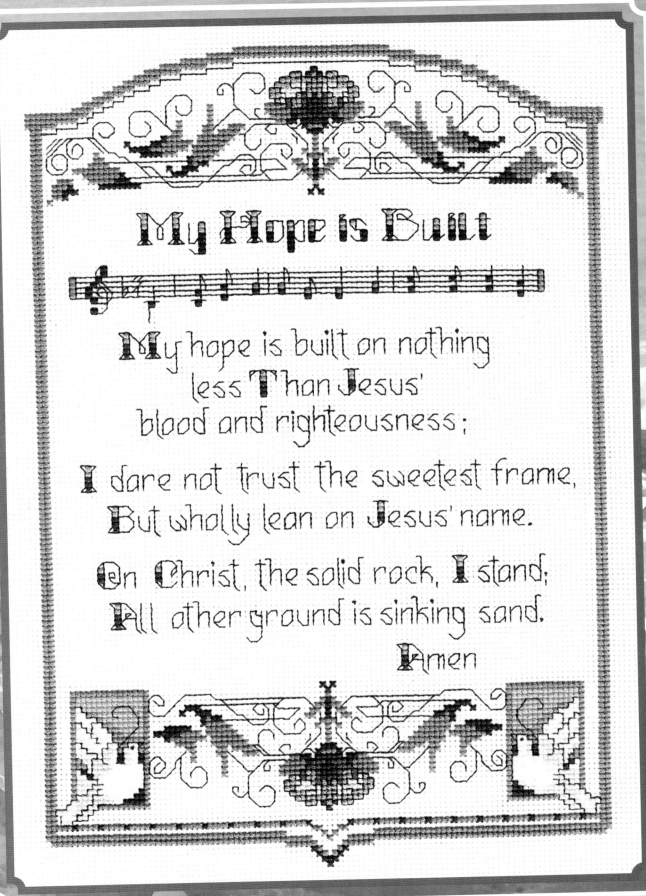

My Hope is Built

My hope is built on nothing
less Than Jesus'
blood and righteousness;

I dare not trust the sweetest frame,
But wholly lean on Jesus' name.

On Christ, the solid rock, I stand;
All other ground is sinking sand.

Amen

Sing Them Over Again to Me

Philip Paul Bliss was a highly gifted musician whose talent defied the poverty and rigors of his youth. He was born in a log cabin in 1838 and was ten years old before he heard the sound of a piano. At the age of eleven, he left home to work at lumber camps and sawmills. Determined to better himself, he attended school whenever work allowed. At seventeen, Bliss was presented with an exciting opportunity—he qualified to became a schoolmaster. J.G. Towner gave him his first formal voice training. In 1859, he wed Lucy J. Young, who encouraged his pursuit of music. Soon, Bliss began writing gospel songs and eventually became an evangelist. Of this hymn he wrote, "I carried that song through two seasons of evangelistic work, never thinking it possessed much merit…it occurred to me to try it one day. To our surprise, the song was received with the greatest enthusiasm." In December 1876, Philip and Lucy Bliss died in a railway accident. Because of his earnest desire to use the gift God gave him, Philip Bliss left behind an enormous musical legacy—a life's work achieved against all odds.

Sing Them Over Again to Me

Sing them over again to me,
Wonderful words of life;

Let me more of their
beauty see,
Wonderful words of life;

Words of life and beauty
Teach me faith and duty.

Beautiful words,
wonderful words,
Wonderful words of life;

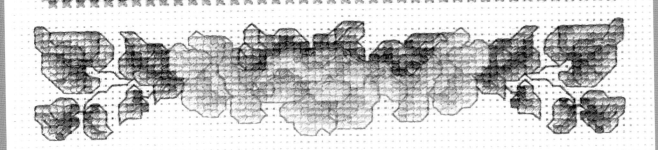

This Is My Father's World

Maltbie D. Babcock was born in 1858 in Syracuse, New York. A young man of many contrasts, Babcock wrote spiritual poetry, loved practical jokes, and was a talented athlete. He was also a brilliant musician. Of the many vocations he could have chosen, young Babcock decided life had most meaning when dedicated to God's service. He became a Presbyterian minister. It became the pastor's habit to take long morning walks. He would call back to his wife as he left the house, "I'm going out to see my Father's world." With this theme in mind, Babcock wrote a sixteen-verse poem praising the glory of creation. Dying unexpectedly at the age of 43, he never had the chance to set **This Is My Father's World** to music. It was his good friend, Franklin L. Sheppard, who adapted an old melody to fit Babcock's words. The hymn is not only a song of praise for the Lord's loving gift of creation, but also a reminder of the glorious future He plans for His children.

❖ This Is My Father's World ❖

This is my Father's world,
And to my listening ears
All nature sings, and round me rings
The music of the spheres.

This is my Father's world:
I rest in the thought
Of rocks and trees,
of skies and seas;

His hand the wonders wrought.

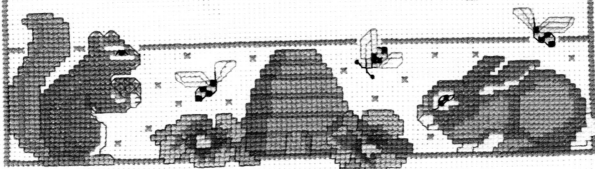

'Tis So Sweet to Trust in Jesus

This lovely song was written by a missionary, Louisa M.R. Stead, who was born in England around the year 1850. As a teen, she felt a strong calling to work in the missionary field. Around the age of 21, she traveled to the United States where she attended a revival meeting that more deeply impressed the call to missions. Around this time, Louisa married and had a daughter. One day, while their little family enjoyed a beachside picnic, Louisa's husband charged into the water to save a child from drowning. It is unclear whether the child was rescued, but it is known that Louisa's husband lost his life in the effort. Without an income, Louisa and her daughter were reliant on the charity of others. It proved to be a time of faith-building. Soon after, she took her daughter with her to South Africa. During her fifteen years as a missionary there, Louisa penned **'Tis So Sweet to Trust in Jesus**. More than a century later, the beautiful words still find a home in the hearts of believers.

Tis So Sweet To Trust In Jesus

Tis so sweet to trust in Jesus,
And to take him at his word;

Just to rest upon his promise,
And to know, "Thus saith the Lord".

Jesus, Jesus, how I trust him,
How I've proved him o'er and o'er!

Jesus, Jesus, precious Jesus!
O for grace to trust him more!

When We Walk with the Lord

In the 1880's, Daniel B. Towner, a trained musician, was assisting the evangelist D.L. Moody at a series of meetings in Brockton, Massachusetts. Towner heard a young man give his Christian testimony, saying, "I am not sure, but I am going to trust, and I am going to obey." Towner was arrested by the simplicity of the statement. He wrote to his friend, the Reverend John H. Sammis, sharing the young man's words. Sammis wrote a poem in reply. Towner began working on music to go with Sammis's poem, but became discouraged and threw it away. Towner's wife found the crumpled piece of paper. She smoothed it out and sang the hymn as she had found it, then encouraged Towner, saying the music was exactly as needed to carry the message. We must suppose that Daniel B. Towner finally agreed with his wife, because generations of the faithful have had the joy of singing the sweet words of the chorus—Trust and Obey.

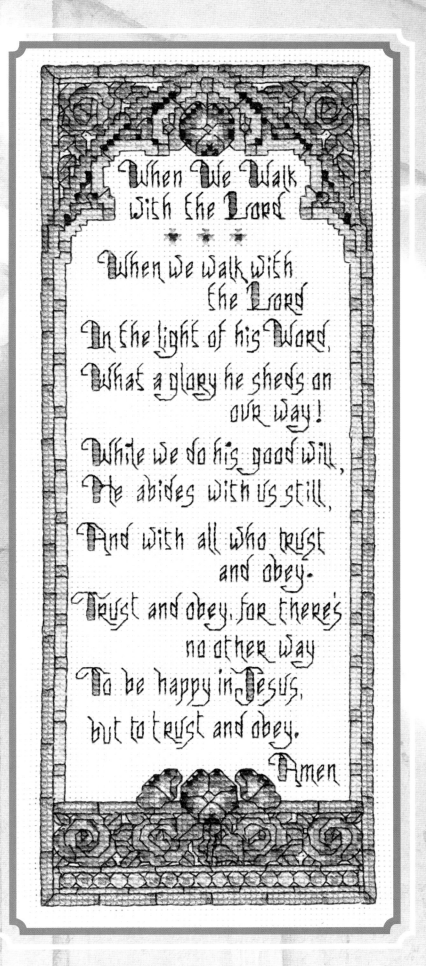

When We Walk
With the Lord

❋ ❋ ❋

When we walk with
the Lord
In the light of his Word,
What a glory he sheds on
our way!

While we do his good will,
He abides with us still,
And with all who trust
and obey.

Trust and obey, for there's
no other way
To be happy in Jesus,
but to trust and obey.

Amen

135w x 160h

DMC	X	FK	BS	Strands	DMC	X	FK	BS	Strands	DMC	X	FK	BS	Strands
223	✚			3	519	✓			3	792			╱	1
319			╱	1	535	■			3	792			╱	2
340	☑			3	535		●	╱	1	793	★			3
341	⊞			3	644	⊔			3	950	◉			3
407	△			3	646	◢			3	3347	♠			3
433		●	╱	1	743	✚			3	3761	⊞			3
472	◇			3	744	☐			3	3772	◆			3
501	▣			3	746	T			3	3854	♥			3
502	⊠			3	792	⬆			3					

Design stitched on 14 count White Aida using 3 strands for cross stitch, 1 and 2 strands for backstitching, and 1 strand for French Knots.

DMC	X	FK	BS	Strands
223	✝			3
319			/	1
340	Z			3
341	I			3
407	△			3
433		●	/	1
472	◇			3
501	⬓			3
502	⧗			3
519	V			3
535	■			3
535		●	/	1
644	L			3
646	◢			3
743	✚			3
744	□			3
746	T			3
792	⬆			3
792			/	1
792			/	2
793	★			3
950	○			3
3347	♠			3
3761	H			3
3772	◆			3
3854	♥			3

111w x 139h

Design stitched on 14 count White Aida using 3 strands for cross stitch, 1 and 2 strands for backstitching, and 1 strand for French Knots.

DMC	X	FK	BS	Strands	DMC	X	FK	BS	Strands
209	H			3	839	■			3
341	Z			3	839			/	1
472	△			3	930	⧗			3
500	◆			3	930		●		1
501	◪			3	930			/	2
501			/	1	931	♥			3
503	□			3	975	L			3
552	◢			3	975			/	1
676	┻			3	977	✚			3
744	4			3	3364	☒			3
746	I			3	3813	V			3

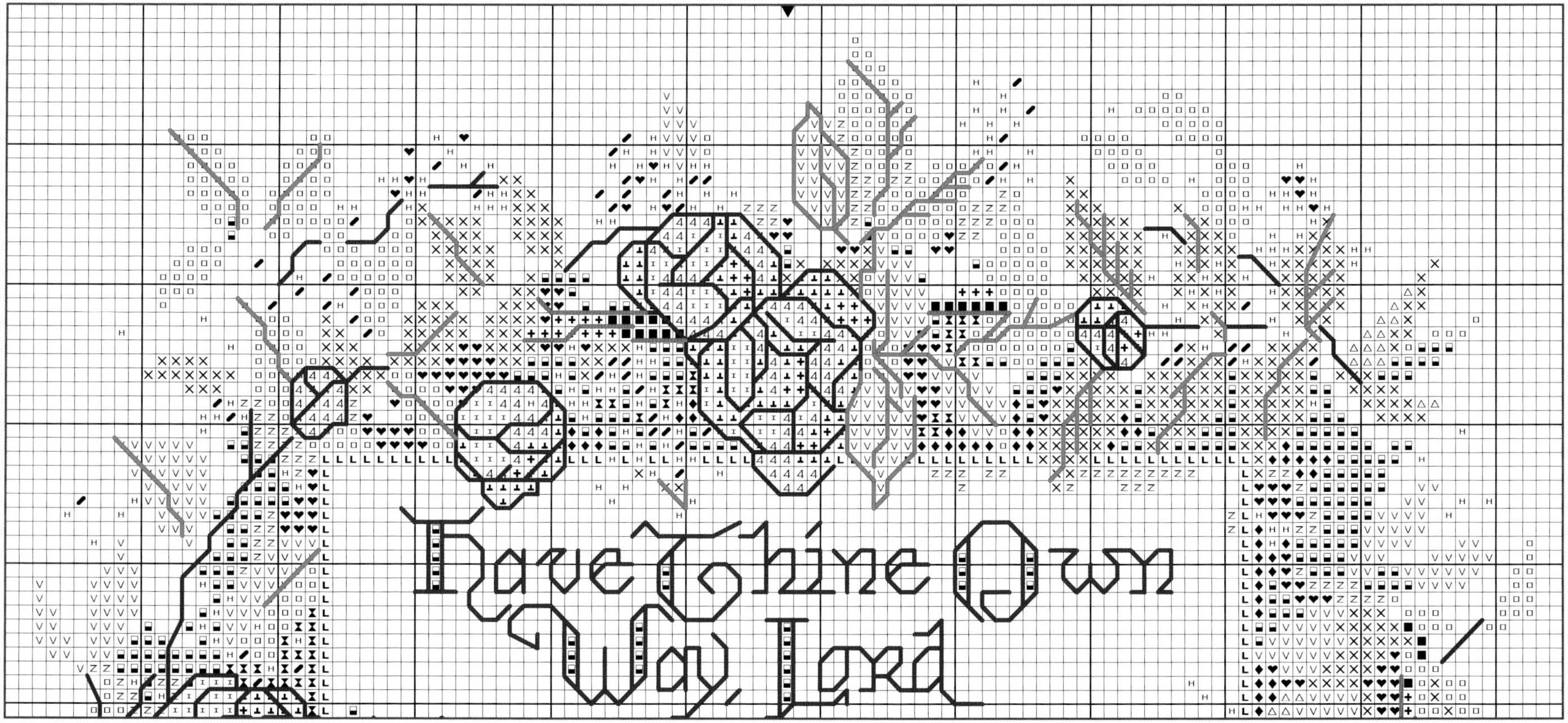

120w x 92h

Design stitched on 14 count White Aida using 3 strands for cross stitch, 1 strand for backstitching, and 1 strand for French Knots.

DMC	X	FK	BS	Strands
white	▫			3
209	▨			3
211	I			3
334	◆			3
340	✖			3
402	◆			3
414	◢			3
415	⊞			3
561	▲			3
563	H			3
603	◣			3
704	Z			3
745	◇			3
747	△			3
762	L			3
912	▪			3
963	⊟			3
975	●			3
3347	◆			3
3799	■			3
3799		●	╱	1
3824	T			3
3826	▐			3
3832	♥			3
3855	★			3
3863	✚			3
3864	V			3

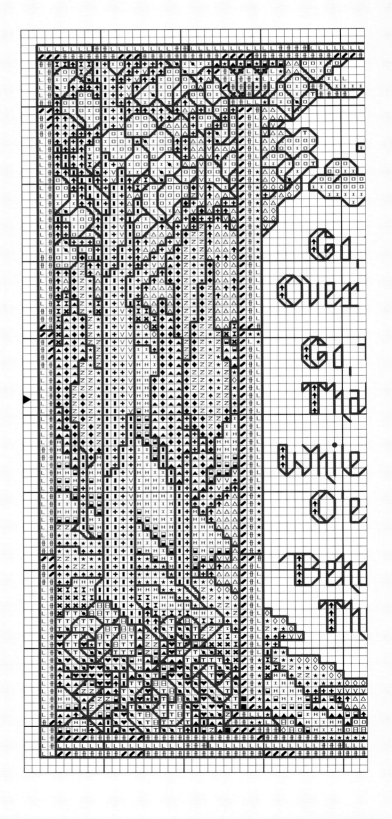

91w x 151h

Design stitched on 14 count White Aida using 3 strands for cross stitch, and 1 and 2 strands for backstitching.

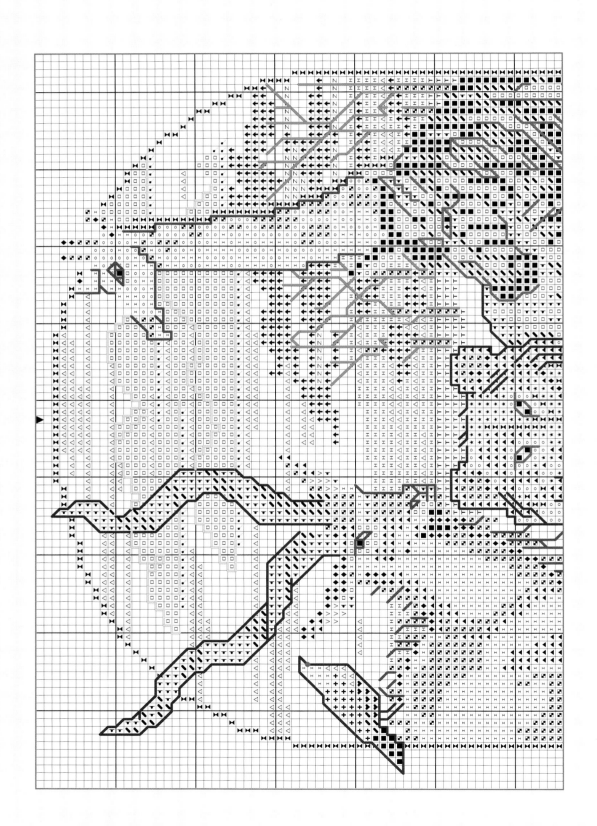

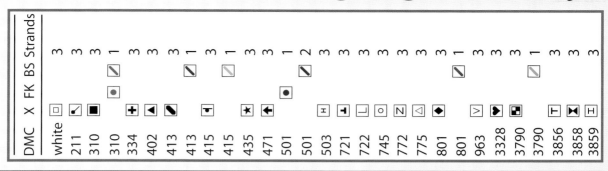

DMC	X	FK	BS	Strands
white	□			3
211	◪		◸	3
310	■			3
310		●		1
334	✚			3
402	◀			3
413	◣		◸	3
413			◸	1
415	▾			3
415		●		1
435	★		◸	3
471	◄			3
501				1
501				2
503	H			3
721	⊢			3
722	∟			3
745	○			3
772	N			3
775	◁			3
801	◆			3
801			◸	1
963	∨			3
3328	▶			3
3790	▣			3
3790			◸	1
3856	⊤			3
3858	⋈			3
3859	H			3

All Things Bright and
Beautiful

All things bright and beautiful,
All creatures great and small,
All things wise and wonderful;
The Lord God made them all.

117w x 143b

Design stitched on 14 count White Aida using 3 strands
for cross stitch, and 2 strands for backstitching.

DMC	X	BS Strands	DMC	X	BS Strands	DMC	X	BS Strands
208	◄	3	793	⊓	3	3722	◥	3
224	◄	3	797	✕	3	3726	►	3
341	H	3	913	◪	3	3727	L	3
420	←	3	937	◆	3	3802	●	3
561	✖	3	989	◔	3	3802	◺	2
729	Z	3	3045	▢	3			
744	T	3	3371	■	3			

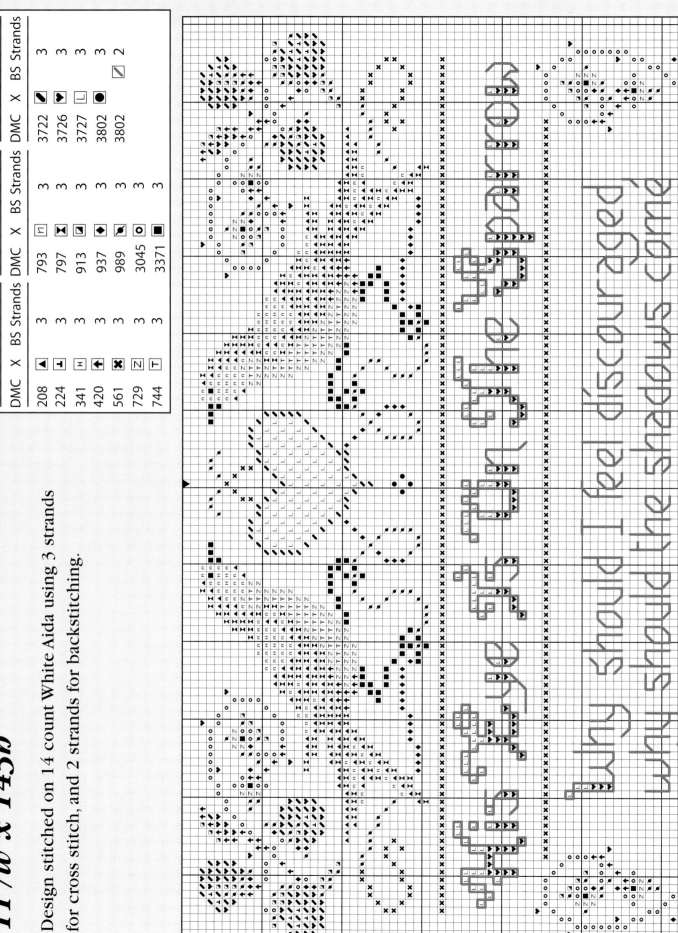

DMC	X	BS	Strands
209	⊠		3
211	T		3
319	▲		3
319		╱	1
333	◢		3
340	Z		3
341	▢		3
472	L		3
552	◆		3
552		╱	1
722	♥		3
738	⊙		3
739	I		3
839	■		3
839		╱	1
839		╱	2
840	▣		3
840		╱	1
841	✚		3
989	☒		3
3363	↑		3
3855	H		3

145w x 116h

Design stitched on 14 count White Aida using 3 strands for cross stitch, and 1 and 2 strands for backstitching.

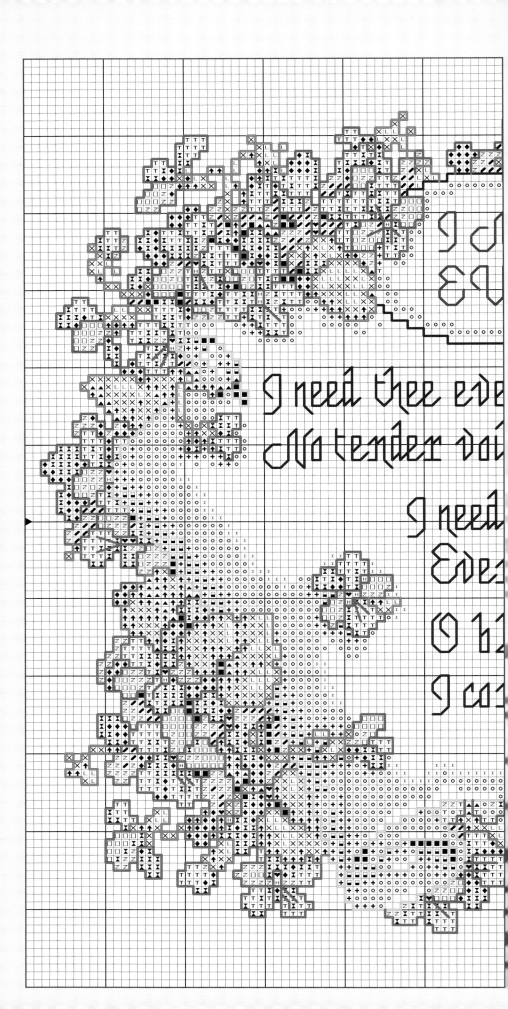

113w x 154b

Design stitched on 14 count

White Aida using 3 strands

for cross stitch, 1 and 2

strands for backstitching, and

1 strand for French Knots.

DMC	X	FK	BS	Strands	DMC	X	FK	BS	Strands	DMC	X	FK	BS	Strands	DMC	X	FK	BS	Strands	DMC	X	FK	BS	Strands
210	⌐			3	335	◥			3	472	○			3	743	⌐			3	962	◑			3
310	■			3	352	◣			3	502	✿			3	745	Z			3	963	H			3
310		●	╱	1	369	T			3	552	◪			3	839	◆			3	3326	☒			3
327		●		1	434			╱	1	553	V			3	931	◀			3	3726	◨			3
327			╱	2	470	◤			3	738	□			3	948	H			3	3813	◇			3
																					3824	◁			3

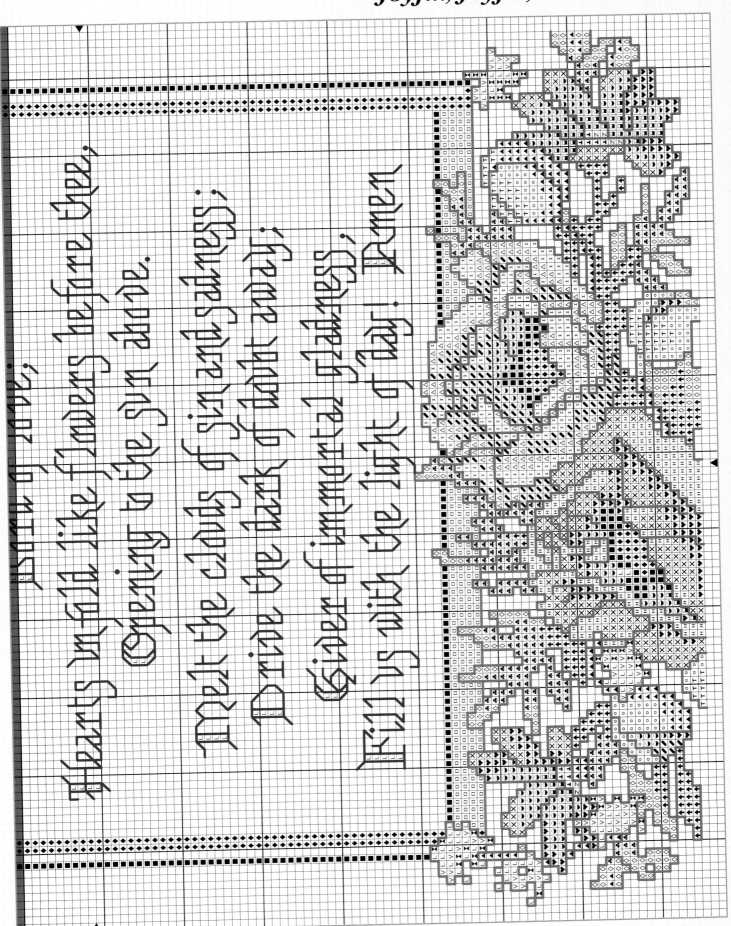

111w x 160b

Design stitched on 14 count White Aida using 3 strands for cross stitch, 1 and 2 strands for back-stitching, and 1 strand for French Knots.

DMC	X	FK	BS	Strands	DMC	X	FK	BS	Strands	DMC	X	FK	BS	Strands
white	□			3	792			◩	1	3051	◥			3
402	◆			3	792		●	◩	1	3051			◿	1
553	←			3	792			◿	2	3053	T			3
747	H			3	794	▣			3	3807	✖			3
										3856	○			3

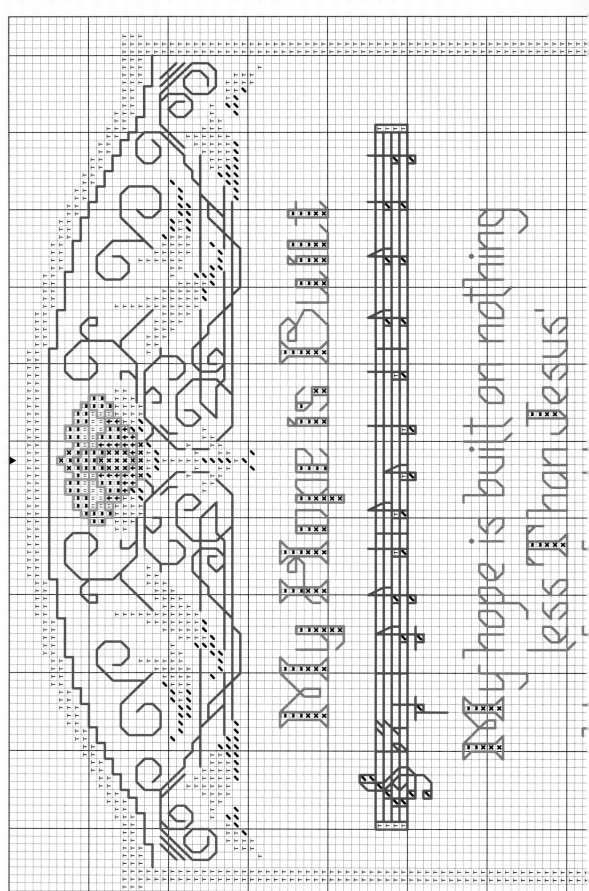

84w x 119h

Design stitched on 14 count White Aida using 3 strands for cross stitch, 1 strand for backstitching, and 1 strand for French Knots.

DMC	X	FK	BS	Strands
335			◩	1
352	◨			3
368	✖			3
369	∨			3
502	⊠			3
745	H			3
754	△			3
818	L			3
948	T			3
962	♥			3
3362		⊙	◩	1
3363	◆			3
3363			◩	1
3716	⊥			3
3776	■			3
3813	Z			3
3822	⬆			3

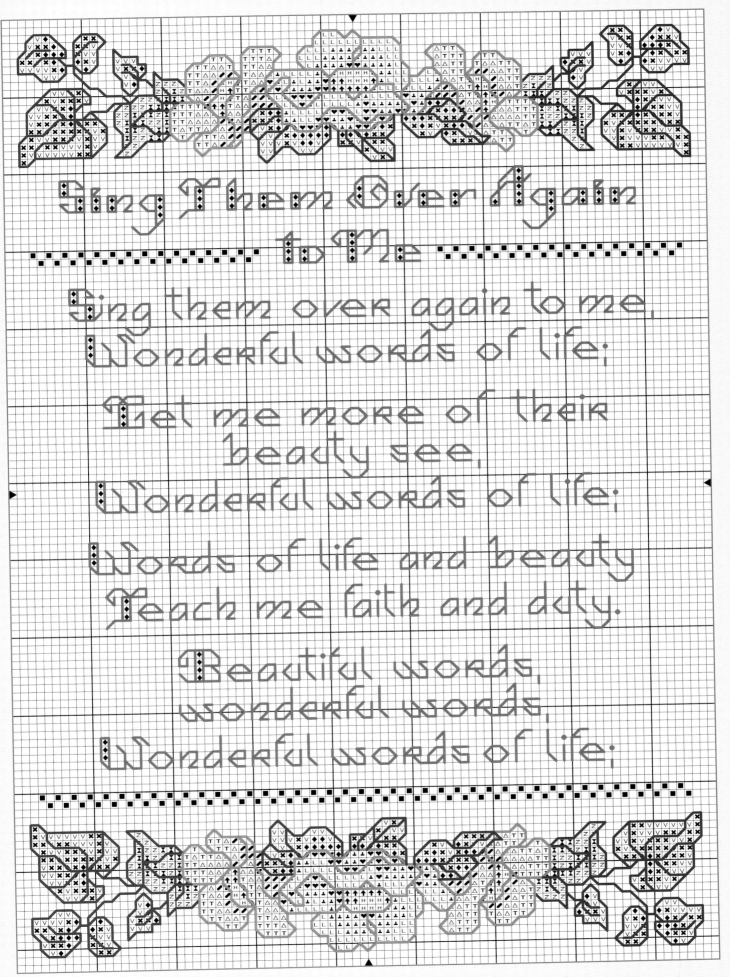

Sing Them Over Again
to Me

Sing them over again to me,
Wonderful words of life;
Let me more of their
beauty see,
Wonderful words of life;
Words of life and beauty
Teach me faith and duty.

Beautiful words,
wonderful words,
Wonderful words of life;

121w x 153b

Design stitched on 14 count
White Aida using 3 strands
for cross stitch, 1 strand for
backstitching, and 1 strand for
French Knots.

DMC	X	FK	BS	Strands	DMC	X	FK	BS	Strands	DMC	X	FK	BS	Strands	DMC	X	FK	BS	Strands
white	□			3	744	✚			3	841	◩			3	950	T			3
210	∨			3	745	H			3	842	◇			3	955	L			3
310	■			3	762	◨			3	920	▶			3	3348	△			3
310		●	◣	1	793	◀			3	920		☑	◥	1	3776	▣			3
319		●	◢	1	793	Z			3	921	✖			3					
327			◣	3	840	◪			3	948	●			3					

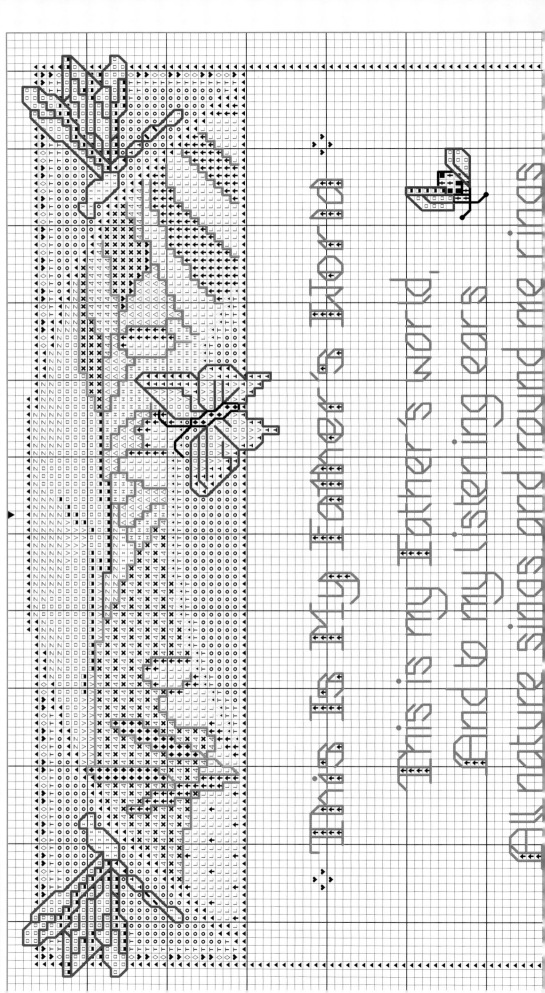

The music of the spheres.

This is my Father's world:

I rest in the thought

Of rocks and trees,

of skies and seas;

His hand the wonders wrought.

114w x 161b

Design stitched on 14 count White
Aida using 3 strands for cross stitch,
1 and 2 strands for backstitching,
and 1 strand for French Knots.

DMC	X	FK	BS	Strands	DMC	X	FK	BS	Strands	DMC	X	FK	BS	Strands	DMC	X	FK	BS	Strands	DMC	X	FK	BS	Strands
310	■	🖉		3	610	◆		✕	3	792	✚			3	827	T			3	3799	◣			3
333	🖋			3	721	✕			3	792		●		1	900	◗			1	3799		●		1
340	◁			3	744	○			3	792			◪	2	976	■			3	3825	H			3
414	H			3	747	☐			3	813	◀			3	977	◀			3					
553	Z			3	780	✚			3	826	★			3	993	◉			3					

52

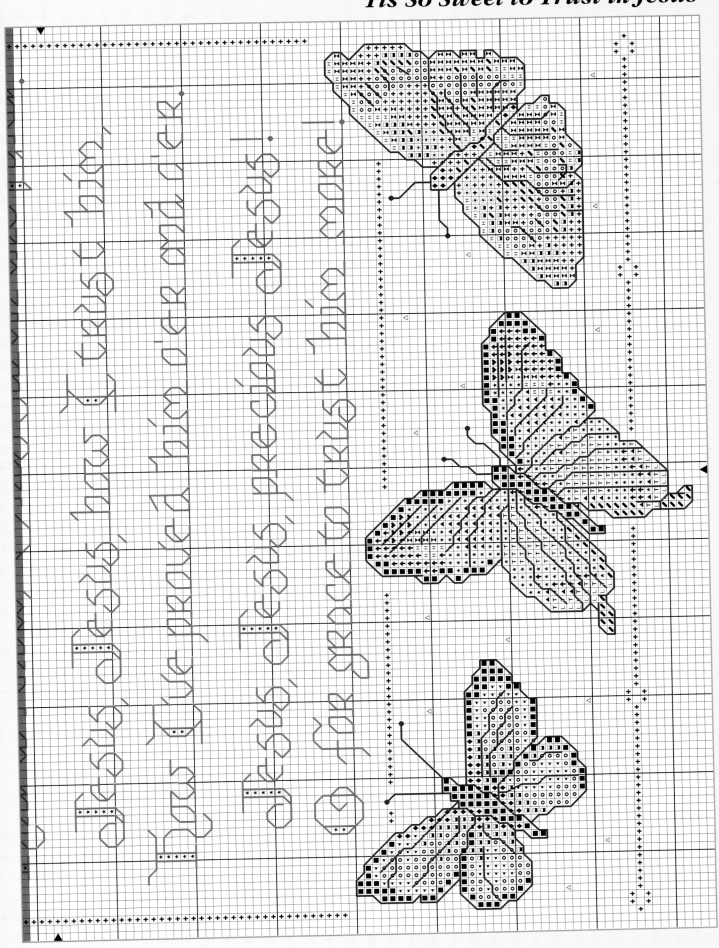

60w x 157b

Design stitched on 14 count White Aida using 3 strands for cross stitch, 1 strand for backstitching, and 1 strand for French Knots.

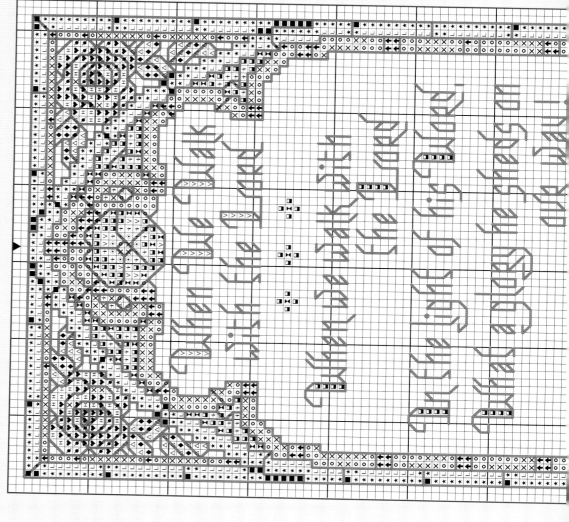

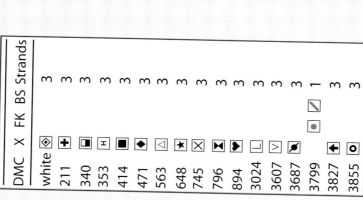

DMC	X	FK	BS	Strands
white	◈			3
211	✚			3
340	◧			3
353	╫			3
414	■			3
471	◆			3
563	◁			3
648	★			3
745	⊠			3
796	⋈			3
894	▶			3
3024	⊔			3
3607	▽			3
3687	◢			3
3799		╱		1
3827	←	●		3
3855	○			3

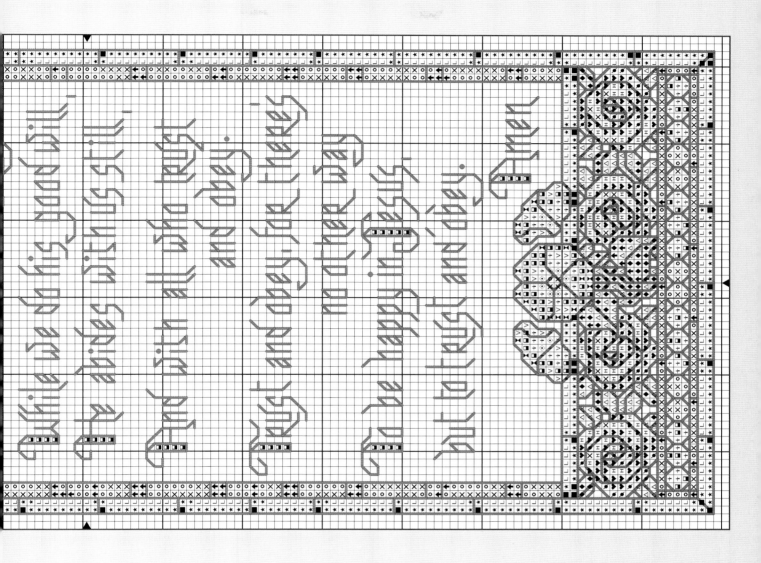

Produced by:
Kooler Design Studio, Inc.
399 Taylor Blvd., Suite 104
Pleasant Hill, CA 94523
info@koolerdesign.com

Production Team:

• Creative Director: Donna Kooler

• Designer: Linda Gillum

• Editor-In-Chief: Judy Swager

• Technical Editor: Priscilla Timm

• Graphic Designer: Ashley Rocha

• Art Director: Basha Kooler

• Photography: Dianne Woods

Published by:

Copyright ©2009 by Leisure Arts, Inc.,
5701 Ranch Drive, Little Rock, AR 72223
www.leisurearts.com